7 Days of
CREATION

A Heart of a Child series
PRAYER & ACTIVITY BOOK

Adiana Pierre

ISBN-10: 1724575465
ISBN-13: 978- 1724575463

PECULIAR TREASURE PRESS
MIAMI

DEDICATION TO

My Lord and Savior for the vision,
My children and inspiration:
Payton D. Pierre & Carter C. Pierre

Hey, Happy Hearts!

Guess what journey we're going on today?

A long time ago, before cars, buildings, planes, toys and playgrounds existed, God did the amazing!

Let's discover together what He did.

In the beginning...

Even before creatures including dinosaurs existed.

Let's Pray Before we continue.

Our Father's Prayer

Matthew 6:9-13

Our Father which art in heaven,
Hallowed be thy name.
Thy kingdom come.
Thy will be done in earth,
as it is in heaven.
Give us this day our daily bread.
And forgive us our debts,
as we forgive our debtors.
And lead us not into temptation,
But deliver us from evil:
For thine is the kingdom,
and the power, and the glory,
Forever.

AMEN.

Day 1

Light from darkness

God said, "let there be light," and there was light.
-Genesis 1:3

Jesus came as light to guide us.
-John 12:46

Now that you have learned about what God did in 7 days,
let's fill in the blanks with what He did each day.

Day 1	
Day 2	
Day 3	
Day 4	
Day 5	
Day 6	
Day 7	

For we are God's workmanship,
created in Christ Jesus
to do good works.
-Ephesians 2:10

POWER
In Prayer!

POWER
In God's
Word!

POWER
In Obedience

POWER
In Love

We need POWER to do
as we were created to do.

Now that you have read John 3:16.

Let's fill in the blanks below.

For God so loved the _____ that He gave his only begotten _____ that whosoever believe in Him shall not _____ but have everlasting _____.

For God so loved _____

Scriptures for You

You don't live by food alone.

Matthew 4:4

Man shall not live by bread alone, but by every word that proceeds out of the mouth of God.

POWER In God's Word!

You are royalty

1 Peter 2:9

But you are a chosen generation, a royal priesthood, an holy nation, a peculiar people...

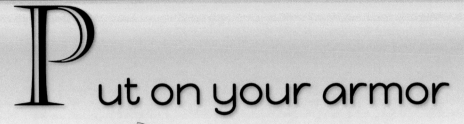

Put on your armor

The full armor of God

Ephesians 6:13-16

- The helmet of Salvation
- The breastplate of Righteousness
- The shield of Faith
- The sword of the Spirit
- The belt of Truth
- Ready shoes of The Gospel of Peace

Why do we need the whole armor?
To be strong in the Lord,
and in the power of His might.

Word Scramble

Before we move ahead,
let's be sure you have on the whole armor of God.

SCRAMBLED	UNSCRAMBLED
INSAALVOT	
SRNISEGHSUOET	
HRUTT	
LOGPES	
HAIFT	
EAPCE	
TRIIPS	

Now, that you're geared up, let's continue.

Always Give Thanks

Psalm 107:1

O give thanks unto the Lord, for He is good: for His mercy endures forever.

POWER In God's Word!

You are the Head

Deuteronomy 28:13

And the Lord shall make you the head, and not the tail; and you shall be above only, and you shall not be beneath.

Children obey

Ephesians 6:1

Children obey your parents in the Lord: for this is right.

What is Obedience?

When I am asked to do something, obedience is doing it right away without needing reminders.

POWER
In Obedience

God knows best.

Bible Word Search

A	G	E	W	U	C	L	H	I	L	U	X	A	E	O	Q
V	S	H	E	P	H	E	R	D	O	L	L	E	I	B	L
B	J	S	G	I	L	E	R	U	N	M	S	L	Y	E	T
T	G	O	N	P	L	S	P	I	R	I	T	S	S	D	U
R	W	I	Q	L	M	U	N	C	E	G	G	D	X	I	D
U	G	P	P	R	A	Y	E	R	G	L	M	N	T	E	W
T	G	D	G	I	R	A	F	C	H	U	R	C	H	N	I
H	O	L	Y	Z	M	P	U	L	A	D	G	J	A	C	K
E	H	K	O	Q	O	S	V	X	Z	P	M	L	N	E	D
W	B	F	H	N	R	O	Y	A	L	R	T	O	K	P	V
H	R	X	Q	Z	C	M	J	G	O	M	A	R	S	D	B

Did you find these words?

1. SPIRIT
2. PRAYER
3. CHURCH
4. SHEPHERD

5. OBEDIENCE
6. HOLY
7. ROYAL
8. THANKS

9. TRUTH
10. ARMOR

Scriptures for You

Joy is strength.

Nehemiah 8:10

The Joy of the Lord is your strength

My Shepherd

Psalm 23

The Lord is my Shepherd

No weapon.

Isaiah 54:17

No weapon formed against me shall prosper.

You have the mind of Christ.

1 Corinthians 2:16

But we have the mind of Christ.

You are an overcomer.

1 John 4:4

Because greater is He that is in you,

than he that is in the world.

You may cry sometimes.

Psalm 30:5

Weeping may endure for a night,

but joy comes in the morning.

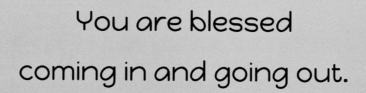

You are blessed

coming in and going out.

Deuteronomy 28:6

Blessed shall you be when you come in, and blessed
shall you be when you go out.

There is power
in being a
Kingdom Kid!

Now that you have learned scriptures,

let's see how much you can remember.

1. The lord is my _____.
2. No weapon formed against me shall _____.
3. The Joy of the Lord is my _____.
4. For God so loved the _____.
5. I am _____ coming in and going out.
6. _____ endures for a night, but joy comes.
7. I have the mind of _____.
8. _____ is He that is in me.

Salvation

Greater

World

Weeping

Strength

Christ

HOLY BIBLE

Blessed

I Love Jesus

Prosper

Scriptures for You

The Fruits

Galatians 5:22

Love, Joy, Peace, Patience, Kindness, Goodness, Faithfulness, Gentleness and Self- control.

Wept

John 11:35

Jesus Wept.

Fruit Tree

Fill in the missing letters.

P ◯ T I ◯ N ◯ E

K ◯ N D ◯ E S ◯

G ◯ O D N ◯ S S

F ◯ I T ◯ F U L

Can you list 5 fruit of the Spirit?

1. _____

2. _____

3. _____

4. _____

5. _____

Rejoice!

Philippians 4:4

Rejoice in the Lord always and again I say rejoice!

(Sing a Song of Praise!)

Job well done!

Sinner's Prayer

Dear Jesus,
I am a sinner
and I need you to save me.
Thank you for dying on the cross
and paying the price for all my sins.
Because of this, I am forgiven.
Please be my Lord and Savior
and help me to live my life for you.
In Your Name, Christ Jesus, I pray.

Amen.

Happy Heart Parents

Train up a child in the way he should go,
And when he is old he will not depart from it.

Proverbs 22:6

Thank you for choosing a Heart of a Child's, 7 days of Creation. Our prayer is that the hearts of every child who reads this book will grow in the goodness of our Lord and Savior Jesus Christ, for His glory.

Remember these POWER points:
- Prayer—talk to God and He will listen.
- Scripture--studying God's Word daily keeps you like a tree planted by rivers of water.
- Obedience - obey God's Word.
- Love—Love God with all of your heart.
- Praise & Worship—rejoice always in giving God thanks for everything.

-Heart of a Child

Made in the USA
Columbia, SC
01 September 2019